Workbook for
The Silva Mind Control Method

By Brighter Health Publishing

Published by Brighter Health Publishing

ISBN: 9798859854387

Printed in the United States of America

Table of Contents

Chapter 1: The Power of Mind Control

Imagine the profound experience of connecting with a pervasive higher intelligence that aligns with you, bringing a sense of joy and affirmation. This connection, achieved through simple methods, banishes the feeling of being out of touch with a hidden wisdom that you always suspected existed but couldn't quite grasp. It feels like a spiritual awakening, evoking awe and wonder. More than half a million people have undergone the Silva Mind Control training, experiencing this transformative journey. By learning and applying these methods, individuals gain newfound powers and energies, leading to a calm, self-confident, and enriched life, free from troubles.

Tap into your mind's full potential

Students are introduced to the idea that they can tap into more of their mind's potential and use it in a unique way. This simple statement holds an astonishing meaning: everyone possesses untapped powers that even beginners doubt until they experience them firsthand. Students are also guided to mentally project themselves to their ideal place of relaxation, a vivid exercise that enhances imagination and promotes deep relaxation. While meditation is commonly understood as thinking things over, Mind Control introduces a specific level of mind where conscious thought is cleared, leading to a calm state that prevents tension-related illnesses. Beyond passive meditation, Mind Control teaches dynamic meditation, enabling the student to solve both minor and major problems using this heightened level of mind. The brain-wave patterns associated with different states of consciousness are explained, with Beta being the awake state, Alpha representing daydreaming or relaxation, and Theta and Delta occurring during sleep. Mind Control training allows individuals to enter the Alpha level consciously while remaining fully alert.

The Alpha Dimension

For many people, their abilities in deeper levels of consciousness are limited due to their conditioning to function primarily in the Beta state. However, through Mind Control training, endless possibilities unfold. The Alpha dimension, with its unique set of sensing faculties, becomes accessible, allowing individuals to tap into Higher Intelligence and operate psychically. While many initially seek Mind Control for relaxation, insomnia relief, or specific goals like weight loss or memory improvement, they discover that they possess innate senses beyond the traditional five. Mind Control's mission is to awaken and train individuals to utilize these dormant powers.

Reflection Questions

What initially drew you to this book? Have you read other books that discuss the power of one's mind?

_____
_____
_____
_____
_____
_____
_____
_____

What is the concept of Mind Control as introduced in Chapter 1, and how does it differ from traditional views of the mind and consciousness?

_____
_____
_____
_____
_____
_____
_____
_____

How does the author describe the different brainwave states (Alpha, Theta, Beta) and their significance in Mind Control?

_____
_____
_____
_____
_____
_____
_____

What do you hope to achieve with Mind Control? Write your goals here:

_____
_____
_____
_____
_____
_____
_____
_____
_____

Chapter 2: Jose SIlva's Story

The development of the Mind Control method

Born in poverty in Texas, Jose Silva took on the responsibility of providing for his family at a young age. Through determination and resourcefulness, he learned to read and write with the help of his siblings and embarked on a self-taught journey in radio repair. Building a successful repair business, he supported his family's education and eventually accumulated funds for his two decades of research that led to the development of Mind Control. His quest for knowledge was sparked by a perplexing encounter with a psychiatrist's questions during World War II, igniting his curiosity about the human mind. Despite lacking formal diplomas, Jose became a renowned scholar, drawing inspiration from the works of Freud, Jung, and Adler. His exploration led him to question whether hypnosis could enhance learning abilities and intelligence. While working as an instructor in the Signal Corps and rebuilding his business, Jose also took on a teaching position at Laredo Junior College, overseeing colleagues and establishing electronics laboratories.

Jose Silva's repair business thrived with the rise of television, leading him to leave his teaching career and focus on his business, which became the largest in town. During his studies in hypnosis and electronics, combined with his children's academic challenges, he revisited the question of improving learning abilities and IQ through mental training. Recognizing the brain's electrical nature, Jose explored the idea of reducing impedance to enhance brain function. Through hypnosis, he discovered that a less active mind could be more energetic and receptive, but independent thought and understanding were also crucial. Consequently, he developed mental training exercises that utilized relaxed concentration and vivid visualization, leading to improved learning outcomes at lower brain frequencies. Jose's breakthroughs included demonstrating that functioning at Alpha and Theta frequencies with awareness was possible, and he even witnessed his daughter reading his mind during a session.

In 1953, Jose contacted Dr. J. B. Rhine about training his daughter in ESP, but received a disappointing response. However, the remarkable improvement in his children's schoolwork caught the attention of neighbors who requested Jose to train their own children. Over the next decade, Jose trained 39 children in Laredo, refining his techniques and achieving consistent results. This marked the development of the first method in history to train anyone in using ESP. Jose's research was self-financed through his electronics business, and today, the thriving Mind Control organization supports further research and expansion. Despite his success, Jose remains a humble individual with a warm smile and a plain, simple demeanor.

Reflection Questions

How did Jose Silva become interested in psychology?

_____

_____

_____

_____

_____

_____

_____

_____

_____

What can you learn from Jose Silva's journey as the creator of The Mind Control Method?

_____

_____

_____

_____

_____

_____

_____

_____

_____

Chapter 3: How to Meditate

In this chapter, we will summarize Jose Silva's own words. He will guide you on the first steps of your Mind Control journey.

I will guide you in learning meditation, which will allow you to tap into your imagination for problem-solving in the future. Although the method I'll teach is slower without an experienced guide, you will have no difficulty with it. Even if you only learn meditation without further problem-solving, you will still experience the calming and beautiful effects it brings. Meditation at the Alpha level frees you from worries and guilt, and as you progress, these negative feelings will dissipate entirely. Through meditation, the body's natural healing mechanisms are activated, allowing it to regain energy and overcome tension.

How to reach Alpha

To reach the meditative Alpha level of mind, follow these simple steps: Upon awakening in the morning, use the bathroom if needed, and then return to bed. Set an alarm for fifteen minutes later in case you fall asleep during the exercise. Close your eyes and direct your gaze upwards, behind your eyelids, at a 20-degree angle. By maintaining your focus and slowly counting backward from one hundred to one at two-second intervals, you will enter the Alpha state effortlessly, even on your first attempt.

In Mind Control classes, students have varied reactions to their initial experience, ranging from finding it beautiful to feeling nothing at all. The difference lies in their familiarity with the Alpha level of mind. This level is somewhat familiar to everyone as we often enter it in the morning upon awakening. If you didn't feel anything during the first exercise, it means you have been in Alpha before without being consciously aware of it. Simply relax, continue with the exercises, and don't question it. While you can reach Alpha on the first attempt with concentration, it takes seven weeks of practice to reach lower levels of Alpha and eventually Theta. Gradually reduce the counting from one hundred to one to fifty to one, twenty-five to one, ten to one, and finally five to one over ten mornings for each level.

Coming out of Alpha

Say the following sentence to properly come out of Alpha:

"I will slowly come out as I count from one to five, feeling wide awake and better than before. One two—prepare to open your eyes—three—open eyes—four—five—eyes open, wide awake, feeling better than before."

Practice session:

Follow the steps above to reach Alpha upon waking. How does the Alpha State feel for you? Does it feel different from your normal state? Was it easy or difficult for you to reach it? Record your impressions here:

_____

_____

_____

_____

_____

_____

_____

_____

Entering Alpha throughout your day

Find a comfortable chair or bed to sit on, ensuring your feet are flat on the floor. Alternatively, you can sit cross-legged in the lotus position. Keep your head balanced and avoid slumping. Begin by focusing on relaxing different parts of your body, starting from the left foot and progressing upwards to the scalp. You'll be surprised by the initial tension you discover. Next, select a spot about 45 degrees above eye level on the ceiling or opposite wall and maintain your gaze until your eyelids feel heavy and naturally close. Commence your countdown from fifty to one. Practice this for ten days, then switch to counting from ten to one for another ten days, and finally settle on counting from five to one. With the flexibility to practice at any time, establish a routine of meditating two or three times a day, allocating approximately fifteen minutes per session.

Practice session:

Follow the steps above to reach Alpha during the day. Is it easier or more difficult than reaching alpha upon waking? Record your impressions here:

_____

_____

_____

_____

_____

_____

_____

_____

Visualization

After reaching your meditative level, the practice of visualization becomes essential in Mind Control. Create a mental screen, resembling a large movie screen, about six feet in front of you, rather than behind your eyelids. This screen serves as a focal point for projection. Start by choosing a familiar object, such as an orange or an apple, and concentrate on projecting that image onto the screen. Each time you reach your level, focus solely on enhancing the image, making it more vivid in three dimensions, full color, and with intricate details. Avoid distractions and maintain singular concentration on the visualization.

Harness the power of your mind with meditation

The brain is often compared to a wandering monkey, lacking control despite occasional moments of brilliance. To harness the power of our minds, we must train our brains to enter the Alpha state and focus solely on creating vivid mental images. Patience is crucial during this exercise as stray thoughts may intrude. Gently push them away and return to the singular object of focus, avoiding irritation or tension that can disrupt the Alpha state. This practice of meditation brings about a profound inner peace and stillness of mind. While the initial experience may be exhilarating, it is important to remember that this journey extends beyond a temporary "trip" and holds the potential for significant personal growth.

Reflection Questions

What are your initial impressions of meditation? If you already have practiced meditating, does this form feel similar or different to what you've done before?

_____

_____

_____

_____

_____

_____

_____

_____

Like most things, it takes a while for meditation to become a habitual practice. How can you ensure that you incorporate it into your daily schedule? Write some ideas here

_____

_____

_____

_____

_____

_____

_____

_____

Imagine that you have completely harnessed the power of your mind. What would that look like? How would you feel? Write some of your thoughts here:

_____

_____

_____

_____

_____

_____

_____

_____

Chapter 4: Dynamic Meditation

Passive meditation can be achieved through various methods such as focusing on visual images, sounds like OM or A U M, the sensation of breathing, energy points in the body, imagining rhythmic drumming, or listening to religious chants. Counting backward is a preferred method as it requires concentration. Once in the meditative level, remaining there passively is not enough; training the mind for organized, dynamic activities yields astonishing results. The significance of visualizing objects on a mental screen becomes evident as it forms a foundation for using meditation dynamically to solve problems.

An experiment in visualization

Before reaching your meditative level, recall a pleasant experience from yesterday or today, briefly reviewing it in your mind. Once in your level, project the complete incident onto your mental screen, vividly remembering the sights, smells, sounds, and feelings associated with it. You will be amazed by the stark contrast between your Beta memory and the enhanced Alpha recall, similar to the distinction between saying the word "swim" and physically experiencing it.

Practice with visualization

Write down what experience you will recreate here:

_____
_____
_____
_____
_____
_____
_____
_____
_____

Think about the experience in your mind. Recreate it briefly.

Now, go into alpha and project the experience onto your mental screen. Try to visualize as many details as possible.

Now, think of the difference between your initial recall and the visualized recall of the experience. How were they different? Record your impressions here:

_____
_____
_____
_____
_____
_____
_____
_____

The value of reaching the meditative level is twofold: it serves as a steppingstone to something greater, and it is valuable in itself. To demonstrate its usefulness, consider a scenario where you are searching for something you own but is not lost. For example, your car keys. By entering your meditative level, recalling when you last had them, and moving forward in time, you can locate them if they are where you left them. (However, if someone else took them, more advanced techniques are needed to address the situation.)

There are four fundamental laws to consider when working with Mind Control:

Desire: You must have a genuine desire for the desired event to occur. Engaging reasonable levels of desire, such as pleasing your boss or finding satisfaction in a task, are more effective than trivial or irrelevant desires.

Belief: It is crucial to believe that the event can reasonably take place. If you hold beliefs that contradict the event, your mind will work against its realization.

Expectation: While desire and belief are passive, expectation introduces dynamics. You must not only desire and believe but also expect the event to happen. Effective visualization and Mind Control techniques can aid in developing this expectation.

Avoid Creating Problems: The law states that you cannot create a problem through Mind Control. It emphasizes the importance of maintaining ethical intentions and aligning with Higher Intelligence. Seeking personal gain at the expense of others will not yield positive results when working dynamically in the Alpha state.

Using visualization to solve your problems

Choose a persistent problem you're facing, like an ill-tempered boss.

Write what problem you are focusing on here:

_____
_____
_____
_____
_____
_____
_____
_____

Once you reach your meditative level, follow these three steps:

(1) Recreate a recent event related to the problem on your mental screen and briefly relive it.

(2) Shift this scene off the screen and replace it with a positive future scenario, where everything about this problem is resolved. (For example, everyone is cheerful and the boss receives good news.) Visualize the solution if you know it.

(3)Counting to five, you will awaken feeling better and confident that you have set forces in motion to create the desired outcome.

Now that you are awakened, record your impressions. How do you feel now that you have visualized the resolution of your problem. Do you believe that the problem will resolve itself? Record your impressions here:

_____
_____
_____
_____
_____
_____
_____
_____

This technique does not guarantee success without any hitches. However, with persistence, you will start experiencing successful outcomes in your problem-solving meditation sessions. These initial successes may be perceived as coincidences, but as you continue practicing, more coincidences will occur. Your ability to believe and expect improbable events will improve over time, leading to increasingly astounding results. Remember to reference your previous successful experiences when working on each problem, gradually replacing them with even better ones as they arise. This continuous improvement is a fundamental aspect of Mind Control.

Reflection Questions

Review the four fundamental rules of Mind Control. Why do you think these laws are important? What truths do they reveal?

_____

_____

_____

_____

_____

_____

_____

_____

Why do you think visualization is so powerful? Have you used this technique before? What were the results?

_____

_____

_____

_____

_____

_____

_____

_____

_____

Why do you think practice is such an important part of Mind Control? How will you incorporate visualization practice into your life?

_____

_____

_____

_____

_____

_____

_____

_____

Chapter 5: Improving Memory

You can improve your visualization and memory with the mental screen technique: If you associate forgotten information with past events, you will be able to easily recall it. "Forgotten" incidents aren't truly forgotten, just temporarily unretrievable.

Let's say you want to remember the name of someone you met at dinner last week. Simply recreate the dinner on your mental screen. As you fill in as many details as you can, you will eventually be able to remember their name. Alternatively, you can create a triggering mechanism that will allow you to access all memories.

Bring together the thumb and first two fingers of either hand and your mind will instantly adjust to a deeper level. Try it now and nothing will happen; it is not yet a triggering mechanism. To make it one, go to your level and say to yourself (silently or aloud), "Whenever I join my fingers together like this"—now join them—"for a serious purpose I will instantly reach this level of mind to accomplish whatever I desire."

Practice the triggering mechanism daily for a week using consistent words. Your mind will form a strong association between joining fingers and reaching an effective meditative state. When faced with difficulty recalling something like a name, avoid forcing it. Instead, relax, realize you have the ability to trigger recall, and let the memory come naturally.

A Denver fourth-grade teacher uses the Mental Screen and Three Fingers Technique to teach spelling, enabling students to remember and spell twenty words weekly. With the same method, the students learn the multiplication table up to 12 within months instead of a year. Similarly, a college student-taxi driver uses the technique to recall directions to old addresses and to help him with his classwork, leading to academic success with all A's and one B in his studies. He also employs Speed Learning and Three Fingers Technique during exams.

Reflection Questions

How can you use the visualization and triggering mechanism in your life to aid with memory? How will enhancing your memory help you in your schooling, job, or relationships?

_____

_____

_____

_____

_____

_____

_____

_____

Triggering Mechanism Practice

For the next week, practice going into Alpha and saying the words "Whenever I join my fingers together like this for a serious purpose I will instantly reach this level of mind to accomplish whatever I desire" while joining your fingers and thumb together.

Do this every day for a week. Keep track of your progress here:

Day 1: _____

_____

_____

Day 2: _____

_____

_____

Day 3: _____

_____

_____

Day 4: _____

_____

_____

Day 5: _____

_____

_____

Day 6: _____

_____

_____

Day 7: _____

_____

_____

Reflect on the experience. Has the triggering mechanism started to work for you? Have you created an association between your fingers and going into Alpha?

_____

_____

_____

_____

_____

_____

_____

_____

The next time you need to remember something, try using the triggering mechanism to help you recall what you already know.

_____

_____

_____

_____

_____

_____

_____

_____

Chapter 6: Speed Learning

In the last chapter, you learned memory techniques such as entering the meditative level, creating a mental screen, and using the Three Fingers Technique for instant recall. Now, as you progress to Speed Learning, you will discover new ways to acquire information that not only enhance recall but also accelerate and deepen your understanding of what you learn.

There are two learning techniques in Mind Control. The first is the Three Fingers Technique, which improves concentration and memory when used during lectures or reading. Students can recall information better at different levels of consciousness. This technique is simple, you have already learned it! Simply join your two fingers and thumb together as you learned in the previous chapter. If you have successfully created an association between this technique and better mind control, then doing this while you listen to a lecture or sit in a meeting will allow you to remember everything that is discussed. You will absorb the information in such a way that when you do need to recall it, simply joining your fingers together again will bring it into you mind.

The second technique involves using a recorder to read and understand complex material at the Beta and Alpha levels for reinforced learning. For example, if you must study and understand a complicated chapter in your textbook, first record yourself reading it aloud in Beta. Then, go into Alpha, and listen to your voice as you read it aloud.

Doing this will help you absorb the information in the deepest possible way. For added reinforcement, let a few days pass and then repeat the process: reading out loud in Beta, and then listening in Alpha. The more you do this technique, the more powerful it will become!

Maybe you are not a student and you are asking yourself if Speed Learning is for you? Anyone who needs to recall information will benefit from the technique. Speed Learning and the Three Fingers Technique offer effective time-saving methods for Mind Control graduates in various fields such as sales, academia, teaching, law, and acting. Insurance agents, lawyers, and comedians benefit from improved recall and understanding of information. Students in multiple educational institutions have also found success, studying less while learning more with these techniques.

Reflection Questions

Think of your day to day activities. Which situations would you benefit from using the Three Finger Technique? How will that help you recall information later on?

_____

_____

_____

_____

_____

_____

_____

_____

_____

Try using the recording method to help you learn a complicated topic. First record yourself reading an excerpt out loud. Then, go into alpha and listen back to the recording of your voice. How does this learning process differ from your usual approach? Do you find it helpful? Reflect on the experience here:

_____

_____

_____

_____

_____

_____

_____

_____

_____

Chapter 7: Creative Sleep

In Mind Control, we view dreams differently than Freud. Rather than exploring spontaneous dreams, we deliberately create dreams to solve problems. By programming their subject matter beforehand, we gain greater control over our lives and find insights and solutions to everyday issues. Dream Control involves three steps, all within a meditational level of mind.

The first step is to recall your dreams. Everyone dreams, even if they don't always remember them the next day. Jose Silva recalls a time when he was engrossed in the psychology of dreams. He fell asleep at 2 AM after a long night of fruitless study. That night he had a significant dream that centered around a source of bright light. He repeatedly saw the numbers 3-4-3 and 3-7-3. The next day, he pondered what the dream could have meant. While shopping with a friend, he came across a lottery ticket with the numbers from his dream. In the end, the ticket ended up winning him 10,000.

But the true value of his dream was much more than 10,000 dollars. To Silva, it was proof that he was one the right track. Somehow he had made a connection with a higher power through his dream. Using mind control techniques, four other mind control students have also won significant sums in lotteries.

Sleep creates favorable conditions for connecting with Higher Intelligence. Dream control consists of a few steps. First, concentrate on learning to recall you dreams. Before you fall asleep say to yourself "I want to remember a dream. I will remember a dream." Fall asleep with a pen and notebook next to you. When you awake, write down everything that you recall from your dream. The more you practice, the easier recall will become.

After you feel comfortable with step one, move on to the following step. Before you fall asleep think of a problem or a question you have. Fall asleep as you say to yourself "I want to have a dream that will contain information to solve the problem I have in mind. I will have such a dream, remember it, and understand it." When you wakeup either at night or in the morning, recall your most vivid dream and search for an answer within.

Using these dream control techniques, you will be able to harness the power of your subconscious.

Reflection Questions

Do you remember your dreams? Do you believe that one can connect with a higher power through dreams?

_____
_____
_____
_____
_____
_____
_____
_____
_____

What kinds of problems would you like to solve through your dreams? Record some of your ideas here:

_____
_____
_____
_____
_____
_____
_____
_____
_____

Turn to the appendix on page 62 for a dream journal that will help you harness the power of your dreams.

Chapter 8: Your Words Have Power

Using your imagination, visualize holding a cold lemon in your hand, examining its yellow skin with small green points. Squeeze it, feel its firmness and weight. Raise it to your nose and smell the unique lemon scent. Cut it in half and notice the stronger odor. Finally, take a deep bite, allowing the lemon juice to swirl in your mouth. If you've immersed yourself in the imagery, your mouth might be watering. This is the power of words. They are so powerful, that the mere suggestion of a lemon can cause your salivary glands to activate.

Words not only reflect reality but also create it, akin to the effect of saliva flow. The brain is a direct receiver and enforcer of our intentions. Mind Control emphasizes "mental housecleaning," being mindful of the words we use to trigger our brains. When we exclaim that something is "a pain in the neck", or that something hurts, we are creating our own negative reality. Good mental housekeeping means changing your thoughts to reflect your desired reality.

As adults, we often use negative words that dull our appetite for life and create negative experiences. The brain responds to these words by manifesting the outcomes we unconsciously order. Repetition and emotional involvement amplify the power of our words. Mind Control provides defenses against these harmful habits, with words having increased power at Alpha and Theta levels. The book has previously shown how simple words can pre-program dreams and enable the Three Fingers Technique to access Alpha state.

Dr. Coue, a chemist from Troyes, France, developed his own psychotherapy based on autosuggestion after studying hypnosis. In 1910, he opened a free clinic in Nancy, successfully treating various ailments. He believed in teaching patients to cure themselves rather than curing them directly. Although the cures were well-documented, the Coue method faded after his death in 1926. Despite its simplicity, anyone can learn it, and the essence of the method lies in Mind Control.

There are two basic principles:

We can only think of one thing at a time

Concentrating on a thought makes it true

Indeed, to trigger the body's healing processes, blocked by negative thoughts, one can repeat the affirmation "Day by day, in every way, I am getting better and better" twenty times, twice a day, using the Coue method. My research has shown that words have even more power at meditative levels like Alpha and Theta. Therefore, we adapt the affirmation to "Every day, in every way, I am getting better, better, and better," repeating it once during meditation. Additionally, we incorporate Dr. Coue's influence with the statement "Negative thoughts, negative suggestions, have no influence over me at any level of mind." These two sentences alone have produced impressive tangible results.

The power of words is evident in the experiences of individuals using simple affirmations. A soldier, unable to complete the full Mind Control course, used only two sentences he learned on the first day to overcome the stress and abuse from his alcoholic sergeant. The affirmations granted him immunity to the sergeant's negativity and cured his newfound coughing and asthma.

Similarly, a nurse anesthetist in Oklahoma, Mrs. Jean Mabrey, utilizes the power of words to help her patients during surgery. By whispering instructions into their ears while they are under anesthesia, she influences their recovery and well-being positively. Patients experience reduced bleeding and faster recovery, transforming their attitudes and improving their overall health. These accounts highlight the remarkable influence words can have on our minds and bodies.

Meet Braylon, The inspiration for the Tale

Braylon is an energetic child who enjoys sports and playing with his brothers. He's allergic to milk, eggs, wheat, peanuts, treenuts and shellfish. He does however love all fruits & veggies as he believes that animals are friends, not food. Braylon's favorite things to do are playing outside and dancing to music. He can't wait to go to school and meet new friends and experience a safe & healthy learning environment outside our house.

(This is my favorite photo of his first bite of an allergy friendly cupcake)

Reflection Questions

Why do you think that words have so much power?

_____
_____
_____
_____
_____
_____
_____
_____

Do you notice that your own words and thoughts have an influence over your life? Write about your experiences here:

_____
_____
_____
_____
_____
_____
_____
_____

How can you harness the power of words and thoughts in your day to day life? Write down your plan here:

_____
_____
_____
_____
_____
_____
_____

Chapter 9: The Power of Imagination

Willpower often falters when faced with tough challenges, but imagination offers a gentler and more effective way to overcome bad habits. True-to-life visualization at deep levels of mind, coupled with belief, desire, and expectancy, can help achieve goals. Emile Coue emphasized that when the will and imagination conflict, the imagination always prevails. To break a bad habit, one must focus on wanting the benefits of giving it up more than the habit itself. Firmly resolving to give up a habit might backfire, just like forcefully trying to fall asleep can keep you awake.

To successfully overcome overeating or smoking using Mind Control, start by reasoning out the problem at the outer level. Determine if your issue is overeating, under-exercising, or both. Consider consulting your physician to identify suitable dietary needs. Understand why you want to lose weight, whether for health reasons or personal attractiveness, and be clear about your desired benefits.

If you eat the right foods in modest amounts, get enough exercise, and are only slightly overweight, it might be unnecessary to pursue weight loss further. Focus your Mind Control on more significant problems or opportunities in your life.

If you genuinely desire to lose weight and have clear reasons, analyze the concrete benefits you'll gain, involving all five senses if possible, rather than vague general benefits. This approach can enhance your motivation and success in achieving your goal. To effectively use Mind Control for weight loss, thoroughly visualize your goal using all five senses and emotions:

Sight: Find a photograph of yourself at your desired weight.

Touch: Imagine how smooth your arms, thighs, and stomach will feel when you achieve your goal weight.

Taste: Visualize the flavors of the foods you will emphasize in your new diet.

Smell: Imagine the pleasant odors of the foods you will be eating.

Hearing: Envision what your loved ones will say about your successful weight loss.

Additionally, imagine the emotions of elation and confidence you will experience when you reach your goal weight. At your meditative level, create your mental screen and project the visualization of your current self, then transition to the future self you aspire to be. Feel and experience every detail of being at your desired weight, including physical actions like bending over, walking upstairs, and fitting into smaller clothing.

Review your new diet, including portion sizes and between-meal snacks. Remind yourself that your body will be satisfied with the provided nourishment and will not send hunger pangs.

Repeat this meditation twice a day to strengthen your focus and motivation towards achieving your weight loss goal.

In the meditation for weight loss using Mind Control, it is essential not to focus on the foods you should not eat. Thinking about those foods might lead your imagination in unwanted directions and hinder your progress. Instead, concentrate solely on the positive aspects of your goal and the benefits you will gain by achieving it.

Hollywood actress Alexis Smith attests to the effectiveness of positive thinking in reducing diets. She emphasizes the importance of not dwelling on what you are giving up but rather concentrating on what you will gain. Alexis attributes her improved attractiveness and better self-control to the practice of Mind Control, which has helped her achieve better balance and control over herself.

In the weight-loss program using Mind Control, it is essential to set a reasonable target for weight reduction to maintain believability and motivation. Unrealistic goals may hinder progress. If cravings for unhealthy foods arise, use the three fingers technique and repeat the same words used during meditation to remind yourself that your diet provides all your body needs, and you will not experience hunger pangs. Glancing at an old photograph of your desired self can also be helpful in reinforcing your commitment.

As you progress with Mind Control, your overall mental state will improve, positively impacting your body's functioning. It will more willingly seek its proper weight with a little mental encouragement.

Various individuals have successfully used Mind Control techniques for weight loss. For example, a man in Omaha developed an interest in healthier foods, leading to a significant weight loss. A woman in Iowa forgot to buy doughnuts for herself due to decreased interest in high-calorie foods. A farmer in Mason City lost 45 pounds and found his ill-fitting suit now appeared tailor-made.

In a workshop for Mind Control graduates, those who genuinely wanted to lose weight experienced an average weight loss of about 4¾ pounds in a month. A follow-up revealed that many continued to lose or maintain their weight. This process was not only painless but joyous, as they reinforced Mind Control-acquired skills without discomfort. The results were similar to successful weight-reduction courses.

Continuing with workshops, the program's organizer, Caroline de Sandre, plans to develop another one for smokers as well. These examples demonstrate the reliability and effectiveness of Mind Control techniques for weight loss and other positive changes.

If you are a smoker, it's time to start becoming a former smoker. Approach this process gradually, giving your body time to adjust to new instructions from your mind. Focus on the benefits of quitting and visualize yourself going through your usual smoking time without smoking, feeling fully at ease and comfortable as a former smoker. Take it step by step, allowing your mind to lead the change through imagination rather than rushing and potentially punishing your body, which is not responsible for the habit.

To control the smoking habit, you can use additional techniques along with the basic method. For instance, a pack-and-a-half-a-day smoker in Omaha visualized all the cigarettes he had ever smoked and burned them in his mind's incinerator. Then, he imagined all the cigarettes he would smoke in the future if he didn't quit and burned those too. After just one meditation session, he quit smoking for good without any cravings, overeating, or side effects.

Reflection Questions:

Think about certain behaviors that you would like to change. Write down a few goals related to them. For example, do you wish to give up smoking? Video games? Are you addicted to your phone?

_____

_____

_____

_____

_____

_____

_____

_____

Now that you have a behavior in mind, try to use the power of your imagination to manifest a change. Write down how you will feel once you have achieved your goal using the five senses:

Sight: _____

_____

_____

_____

Touch: _____

_____

_____

_____

Taste: _____

_____

_____

_____

Smell: _____

_____

_____

_____

Hearing: _____

_____

_____

_____

Now use your mental screen to visualize yourself now followed by yourself once you have achieved your goal. Focus on all five senses plus the emotions that will accompany the achievement of your goal. The more detailed your visualization, the more empowered you will become to change.

Repeat these steps for all your desired goals.

Chapter 10: Using Your Mind to Improve Your Health

As Jose Silva travels and addresses groups of Mind Control graduates, he is amazed at the wonderful self-healings they report. It is astonishing that more people have not recognized the power of their minds over their bodies. While medical research explores the body-mind relationship, we know enough to strengthen the body's repair forces through our minds for more successful combat against illnesses. Even simple methods like Emile Coue's work, but Mind Control's methods are even more powerful. Graduates have used Mind Control in emergencies to reduce bleeding and pain with remarkable results. It is too early for physicians to retire, but as you develop self-healing skills, you may require less medical attention and amaze them with the speed of your recovery.

In self-healing, follow these six steps:

1. Begin in Beta, cultivating love and forgiveness as an end in itself.
2. Go to your level to neutralize negative thoughts and allow the body to repair itself.
3. Mentally express your desire for a mental housecleaning and positive thinking.
4. Briefly mentally experience the illness troubling you to focus your healing energies.
5. Erase the image of the illness and imagine yourself completely cured, feeling the freedom and happiness of perfect health.
6. Reinforce your mental housecleaning and repeat the affirmation, "Every day in every way I am getting better, better, and better."

The self-healing exercise should take about fifteen minutes, and you can do it as often as possible, at least once a day. There is no "too much" when it comes to self-healing and Mind Control's involvement with the world, not withdrawal from it. You can practice step one (cultivating love and forgiveness) in Beta, Alpha, and Theta and use your three fingers for instant reinforcement if needed. Many Mind Control centers have newsletters with countless reports of graduates experiencing improvements in various health conditions.

A practicing physician suffered from severe migraine headaches for years, trying various treatments without success. A Mind Control graduate recommended the practice, and after taking the course, the headaches improved significantly. Although there were occasional relapses, the person continued to use Mind Control techniques, gradually reducing the frequency and intensity of the headaches until they eventually disappeared completely. Since starting Mind Control, they have not needed any aspirin or medication for headaches.

For twenty-seven years, the Sister Barbara Burns of Detroit, Michigan had worn glasses due to nearsighted astigmatism. Through Mind Control, she started visualizing her eyes focusing accurately like a camera lens whenever she blinked. After two weeks of repeating this in meditation, she began to live without glasses for distance vision. She still needed glasses for reading, but she added a cornea correction to her meditation for a few weeks before another examination by an optometrist (who was also a Mind Control graduate). Upon examination, it was found that her vision problems had resolved themselves.

Dr. O. Carl Simonton, a cancer specialist trained in Mind Control techniques, studied spontaneous remissions in cancer patients who recovered without known medical reasons. He found that these patients often had a common trait: they were positive, optimistic, and determined. In his research, he identified significant emotional factors, particularly a major loss experienced six to eighteen months prior to the cancer diagnosis. The way the loss was received by the individual, causing feelings of helplessness and hopelessness, seemed to lower the patient's resistance and contribute to the development of malignancy. Dr. Simonton adapted Mind Control techniques to help cancer patients by fostering a positive mindset and empowering their will to fight the disease.

Dr. Carl Simonton and Stephanie Mathews-Simonton have achieved remarkable results in cancer control by combining visualization for physiological self-regulation with traditional radiology. They train patients to participate mentally in their treatment at the Cancer Counseling and Research Center in Fort Worth. Dr. Simonton believes a patient's attitude can influence disease progression and that Mind Control concepts, including biofeedback and meditation, are powerful tools to teach patients how to be involved in their health process emotionally. They emphasize banishing fear and changing the negative mental image of cancer cells. Rather than viewing cancer cells as all-powerful, they educate patients about the body's natural ability to recognize and destroy cancerous cells. They aim to empower patients to understand that cancer is a normal process and assist the body in regaining control of its natural healing processes.

Reflection Questions

Why do you think that positivity and optimism are associated with better health outcomes?

_____

_____

_____

_____

_____

_____

_____

_____

Can you think of a specific time that positivity and optimism helped you or someone else heal?

_____

_____

_____

_____

_____

_____

_____

_____

How can you use the steps outlined in this chapter to heal yourself? Write about you current health issues here:

_____

_____

_____

_____

_____

_____

_____

_____

Now imagine that you are completely healed. What would that look like? What would that feel like?

_____

_____

_____

_____

_____

_____

_____

_____

Reflection Questions

Why do you think that intimacy is so important for relationships?

_____

_____

_____

_____

_____

_____

_____

_____

_____

Think about your own relationship, or a future relationship. What does intimacy look like to you? How can you become a better partner using mind control?

_____

_____

_____

_____

_____

_____

_____

_____

_____

Chapter 12: You Can Practice ESP

ESP, or extrasensory perception, is widely accepted as real, supported by statistical evidence showing information can be obtained beyond the five senses. In Mind Control, it is referred to as "Effective Sensory Projection," where individuals project their awareness to access desired information. Mind Control trains people to function psychically, allowing them to enter deep levels of consciousness and visualize events vividly. Through intensive training, students can project their awareness outside their bodies and access information in unconventional ways.

In Mind Control training, students practice "Effective Sensory Projection" by projecting their awareness to different locations and dimensions. They mentally explore objects like walls, metal cubes, and living matter, even entering the brain of a pet. They then construct a psychic laboratory, equipped with symbolic instruments to correct abnormalities in humans they will examine the following day. These instruments are highly instrumental symbols tailored to each individual. The students receive inner counsel through a strong, guiding voice during their psychic work.

In the Mind Control laboratory, students evoke two counselors, who may appear as real people, archetypal figures, or inner voices. These counselors offer guidance and practical advice. One student met a clown-like figure and William Shakespeare as counselors. When working with counselors, the association is respectful and invaluable.

These counselors hold the potential to benefit both the student and others. The next day, the students feel immense anticipation as they prepare to perform their psychic work, which will now be witnessed by others. The training has been leading up to this moment, where students can demonstrate their psychic abilities.

In the Mind Control training, students pair off, with one as the "Psychorientologist" and the other as the "psychic operator." The Psychorientologist writes details about a person on a card, and the psychic operator, in a meditative state, visualizes and examines that person's body, seeking to identify any afflictions.

During the session, the psychic operator describes the areas of attraction they sense and consults with their counselors for guidance. They report their findings, even if they feel like they are guessing. Over time, the psychic operators improve their accuracy and begin making direct hits on the afflictions. Although it may seem crazy, many students experience real and accurate psychic insights, proving the efficacy of Mind Control training.

The imagination, when trained, can produce works of art and psychic results. In Mind Control, students initially feel they are "just imagining," but after experiencing accurate hits, they learn to trust their psychic gift. Our minds can reach beyond our heads and tap into ESP, but belief and expectancy are essential motivators.

Students may start with low expectancy, believing ESP is someone else's ability. However, once they achieve their first hit, their expectancy increases, and they become Mind Control graduates. Examples of correctly diagnosing illnesses showcase the power of psychic abilities. Sometimes, apparent misses can be hits on the wrong target, but with practice, accuracy improves, and psychics can connect with objects as well as people.

Psychic energy is strongest when people's survival is at risk, explaining why many spontaneous ESP cases involve accidents and sudden death.

To develop sensitivity and accuracy, Mind Control graduates work with severely ill individuals. By practicing case work, they learn to pick up weaker psychic signals, enabling them to connect with anyone in mind, regardless of their situation.

Children demonstrate psychic abilities more readily than adults due to their open-mindedness and less restricted sense of reality. Early experiments involved separating children and having one create something in their imagination while the other tried to discern their thoughts.

Working at a subtle level requires practice to "become as little children" and tap into psychic abilities more effectively. The next chapter will outline exactly how to practice activiating your own psychic abilities.

Reflection Questions

Why do you think that children naturally have stronger ESP than adults?

_____
_____
_____
_____
_____
_____
_____
_____

Think about your own experiences with ESP. Have you ever had someone accurately intuit something about you? Have you ever accurately guessed something about someone else? Write about your experiences here:

_____
_____
_____
_____
_____
_____
_____
_____

It is normal for people to be skeptical about psychic abilities. Ask yourself if you want to overcome your own skepticism in order to access your natural psychic abilities. Write your thoughts about it here:

_____
_____
_____
_____
_____
_____
_____
_____

Chapter 13: Form Your Own Practice Group

Once you have decided that you want to access your own ESP, it will be helpful for you to form a practice group with at least six people.

Once everyone has mastered the exercises in this group, meet together to begin case work. Everyone should bring four notecards with the name and location of a sick person on one side and the nature of the sickness on the other.

First you will practice mentally projecting yourself into metal objects. You can use dimes, pennies or gold rings. Go in to alpha, then visualize the object in your mind a few feet in front of you and above eye level. Imagine the object expanding and then filling up the entire room. Visualize yourself entering the object. Do this same thing for other objects, such as fruits, vegetables and finally a pet. The important thing is that you get a distinct feeling for each different object.

Before beginning the case work, agree as a group that there will be no ego trips and that success does not equate to superiority. Some may progress faster than others, but the slowest learners can often become the best psychics.

Once you are ready to begin, pair off into groups. One person is the psychic operator, the other is the orientologist. The psychic operator, after hearing the name and location of the sick person, should go into alpha and visualize the person and the illness on their mental screen. Just like with the practice objects before, they should visualize themselves entering the mind of the person. Then, following their overall impressions, they should try to guess the nature of the illness.

The more you practice, the more accurate your guesses will become. Switch off between being the psychic operator and the orientologist.

Some tips for successful practice:

- If you know a Mind Control graduate, invite them to join your group. They can provide valuable guidance and assistance.
- As the psychic, trust your hunches and impressions. Don't try to reason out your findings, and keep talking as you scan the body and describe what you see.
- As the orientologist, refrain from hinting or telling the psychic they are wrong. Be patient and supportive, and avoid discouraging words.
- Keep the group together and continue working cases regularly. With practice, you will become more sensitive and proficient in psychic detection.
- Do not use anyone present in the group as a case, as diagnosing in-person is legally restricted. Stick to working on cases at a distance.
- If you discover an abnormality in a case, do not rush to inform the person. Leave the medical diagnosis to licensed professionals and focus on correcting mentally what you detect.

Reflection Questions

What are the benefits of practicing Mind Control techniques with a partner or in a group, as opposed to doing it alone?

_____

_____

_____

_____

_____

_____

_____

_____

How do the exercises in the book progress from simple visualizations to more complex case work with severely ill people? What is the significance of this progression?

_____

_____

_____

_____

_____

_____

_____

_____

Silva highlights the importance of imagination and trusting the first thing that comes to mind. How does this relate to developing psychic abilities?

_____

_____

_____

_____

_____

_____

_____

_____

What are some potential challenges you may face when practicing case work and psychic detection?

_____
_____
_____
_____
_____
_____
_____
_____
_____

Ask yourself why you want to develop ESP. What are your motivations?

_____
_____
_____
_____
_____
_____
_____
_____
_____

Chapter 14: How to Help Others with Mind Control

Detecting illnesses in unseen persons is astonishing, but it doesn't end there. In addition to detecting, we can project healing energy into their bodies using our intentions. By shifting our intentions from gathering information to healing, we alter the energy's effects.

To link intentions with this healing energy, we visualize the desired conditions without abnormalities, a process known as psychic healing. This can be accomplished even in the early stages of meditation and visualization.

Becoming an effective psychic healer doesn't necessarily require mastering the technique of working cases; using the mental screen for problem-solving can be sufficient. Delaying psychic healing until mastering Mind Control would result in missed opportunities to help others and positively impact their lives.

Before developing Mind Control, Jose Silva began healing work, experimenting with various methods and achieving significant healings, gaining renown as a healer in their region. An early healing involved a parish priest suffering from knee swelling and discomfort. The priest was initially skeptical of the author's parapsychology approach, but later, after researching it, he allowed the author to try healing him. The healing, conducted through mental means, resulted in a miraculous improvement in the priest's condition.

Before healing the priest, Silva engaged in a confident and relaxed conversation, discussing topics that boosted the priest's confidence in parapsychology. During the talk, he visualized the priest's improved health and developed a strong affection for him. Later, at home, the author transferred psychic energy to the priest by holding their breath while envisioning him in perfect health, using the power of focused intention.

In the updated healing method, use the mental screen vividly and confidently. Begin by projecting the person and their ailment onto the screen, then visualize a corrective action to the left. Finally, project a vivid image of the person in perfect health and happiness even further left. Believe that this happy image is already real, as your mind is in league with causes at Alpha and Theta levels. Visualize the results as already achieved, rather than becoming real in the future. This approach is more effective and easier for the healer.

The universe guarantees that all individuals can cause lawful things to happen through their desire, belief, and expectancy. When visualizing a person's perfect health, there comes a pleasant feeling of accomplishment. With practice, more beautiful coincidences occur, reinforcing belief and sparking a chain reaction. While faith and psychic healing techniques may differ, their principles and results are similar. Mind Control methods have a positive effect on the healer, leading to a sense of accomplishment and feeling better after healing sessions.

Many healers believe they cannot heal themselves and fear losing their power if they try. However, we have proven this belief to be untrue through Mind Control practices. Many also think they must be physically present for healing, but absent healing has been shown to work effectively. Christ's healing of the Centurion's servant from a distance serves as an example. There is wisdom in keeping healing visualizations private, as it helps conserve and amplify the energy directed towards the healing intention. Thus, keeping healing work to oneself can be beneficial, as seen in Christ's instructions after one of His healings.

Reflection Questions

Think about the implications of healing others through Mind Control. How does it make you feel to know that helping others is a possibility?

_____
_____
_____
_____
_____
_____
_____
_____

Silva mentions that one should not delay psychic healing just because one has not completely mastered Mind Control. Why do you think that is?

_____
_____
_____
_____
_____
_____
_____
_____

How can you use what you've learned so far to help someone you know? Think of someone who needs either mental or physical healing and visualize them now in perfect health. Write about what perfect health would mean for that person.

_____
_____
_____
_____
_____
_____
_____

Why is it sometimes beneficial to keep healing work to oneself?

_____

_____

_____

_____

_____

_____

_____

_____

Chapter 15: Some Speculations

The chapters from 3 to 15 of this book, as well as the Mind Control course, aim to help readers tap into more of their mind's potential to solve various life problems. Silva's work is rooted in over thirty years of study and experimentation, approaching practical issues due to his humble beginnings. Despite the astonishing discoveries, he found that none of the techniques conflicted with his religious beliefs or any other established worldview. Mind Control has proven to be beneficial for people of various religious backgrounds and even atheists, scientists, and scholars. While the techniques themselves may be neutral the author firmly believes that Mind Control holds inherent positive values, supported by logical reasoning.

The universe operates under laws, which science continues to explore and understand.

We cannot break these laws; our actions may lead to consequences, but the laws themselves remain intact.

It is reasonable to consider that the universe can think about itself, given our own capacity for self-awareness.

The universe is not indifferent to us; as part of it, it responds to our actions and intentions.

In our truest state, such as during meditation, we are fundamentally capable of doing no harm and can bring about significant good.

Reality is often described as a shared dream, and our perception of it is shaped for convenience. Everything is energy, with differences in frequency defining various forms. Thoughts can influence things and events since thoughts are a form of energy. Time presents different perspectives, with the straight-line concept being practical for everyday living. However, in states like Alpha and Theta, we can access past and future events through precognition, suggesting that time itself may be a form of energy.

Reflection Questions

Now that you have read about the basics of Mind Control, do you believe that your thoughts have the power to influence reality?

_____

_____

_____

_____

_____

_____

_____

_____

_____

Chapter 16: Your Self-esteem Will Soar

The Mind Control Method has transformative effects on individuals' self-esteem and self-guidance. Singer-actress Carol Lawrence and others testify to the empowering nature of the program. Studies conducted in various educational settings, including colleges, high schools, and elementary schools, reveal consistent and predictable improvements in ego strength and self-assurance among students. These findings indicate that Mind Control fosters a greater sense of self-respect and confidence, leading to positive changes in individuals' lives.

Mind Control produced significant positive changes in ego strength and composure at Hallahan High, Lawrenceville, and St Fidelis schools. These improvements far exceeded what could occur by chance alone. The study demonstrated that Mind Control training had a lasting impact on students' self-assurance and ability to manage emotions, as evidenced by their continued positive results four months after the training.

There are countless studies that outline the ways in which the Mind Control Method can help individual's overcoming difficulties like addiction and illness.

A halfway house used the Mind Control Method to help residents with serious substance abuse issues.

Fifteen new Mind Control graduates at the halfway house were followed up six months later:

Subject 1: No relapse, improved personality.
Subject 2: No relapse, developing a sense of well-being and self-confidence.
Subject 3: No relapse, showing progress in A.A. program.
Subject 4: No relapse, Mind Control reinforced therapeutic treatment.
Subject 5: No relapse since hospital discharge.
Subject 6: No relapse, improved family and college grades.
Subject 7: No relapse, living the A.A. philosophy.
Subject 8: No relapse, improved family relations and temperament.
Subject 9: No relapse, currently employed.
Subject 10: No relapse, goal-oriented and seeking higher achievement.
Subject 11: No relapse, life progressively getting better in work and family.
Subject 12: One brief relapse, overall positive progress.
Subject 13: No relapse, getting life together with improvements in work and family.
There are many more examples of the empowering nature of the Mind Control Method. It's application has many powerful uses that can be unlocked with practice and time.

Reflection Questions

Why do you think that the mind Control method is so powerful for one's self-esteem?

_____

_____

_____

_____

_____

_____

_____

Have you seen any boosts in your own empowerment as you've learned about Mind Control?

_____

_____

_____

_____

_____

_____

_____

_____

How can you use Mind Control to boost other's self-worth?

_____

_____

_____

_____

_____

_____

_____

Chapter 17: Mind Control in the Business World

Imagine believing in Murphy's Law, that everything that can go wrong will go wrong at the worst time, and then discovering the cosmic Bill of Rights from Jose's teachings: "You feel luckier because you are luckier."

.Mind Control graduates report feeling luckier and experiencing positive changes in their lives. At Hoffmann-La Roche, Inc., a pharmaceutical company, employees took the Mind Control course to achieve better mental health and increased effectiveness. Over three hundred graduates, including top executives, scientists, and personnel managers, found the course transformative. Graduates mentioned improved awareness, positive thinking, better interactions with colleagues, and increased confidence as valuable outcomes of the program.

Mr. Herro, interested in Mind Control's usefulness in business and sports, facilitated several Chicago White Sox players taking the course, leading to significant improvements in their performance. Salesmen are among the most enthusiastic graduates, using visualization techniques to achieve remarkable results in their work. A vice-president of a steel company recommends Mind Control to others, believing it benefits both work and personal life.

Mind Control training has shown impressive results in helping graduates find new jobs. The increased self-assurance and calmness from the training contribute to better job interviews and career prospects. Many individuals have experienced positive shifts in their careers after using Mind Control techniques. For instance, a photographer who lost his job found new opportunities by visualizing himself attending college and securing a better job. Another graduate in New York landed a job paying three times more than his previous one after using the techniques. In a unique example, a couple who open safes for a living use Mind Control to recall combinations for grateful owners who have forgotten them.

Chapter 18: Where Do We Go from Here

After experiencing success with Mind Control, you'll embark on a journey of self-discovery with all positive outcomes. Different paths will be open to you: exploring more techniques, specializing in one that works best, or drifting away from practice. While seeking additional techniques may yield results, it might divert your focus from mastering the essential ones. Drifting away is common, but the training is never completely lost and can be recalled in emergencies. The best approach is to embrace the complete set of Mind Control techniques, as they reinforce each other and lead to truly full development. The course and Jose's teachings are interconnected, and the synergy of all techniques creates a greater whole.

After mastering the basic techniques of Mind Control, there are still further levels of control and subtleties of experience to explore. The ultimate realization comes when you can turn all your problems into projects and make them work out as desired. This goes beyond simple achievement; it is a profound understanding of the enormous powers we possess and the responsibility to use them constructively. Through Mind Control, this depth of experience allows you to recognize a benevolent purpose behind everything and a sense of dignity and purpose in our presence on this planet. This realization comes not through mystical experiences but from the practical application of Mind Control techniques in daily life, shaping both the everyday details and the destiny of your journey.

In this small incident, a new Mind Control graduate experienced a moment of doubt when he couldn't find a second roll of film in his luggage, even though he vividly remembered putting it in. Despite the coffee-table scene repeatedly appearing on his Mental Screen, he persisted and eventually realized there never was a second roll. This small event served as his first concrete evidence of having more confidence in his own mind.

As he continues practicing Mind Control and encounters more incidents like this, his self-view and perspective of the world will gradually shift. Along the way, he may also achieve significant results, such as helping his allergic daughter overcome her allergy to cats through visualization and meditation. These experiences will lead him to a deeper understanding of the powers within himself and the purpose behind his presence in this world, eventually leading to a firm certainty and a transformed life.

With consistent practice of Mind Control, your mind becomes more attuned and sensitive to subtle signals on important matters. It starts to take shortcuts and can pass on valuable information without you actively searching for it. A Mind Control graduate experienced this when, during her meditation, a large black X appeared on her Mental Screen, blocking out scenes related to her office. This strong intuitive feeling urged her to avoid going to her office that day, and she listened to it, staying home instead. Later, she discovered that her office was targeted in an armed robbery, and several people were badly injured. Her Mental Screen provided her with a life-saving hunch that she would normally get through Dream Control.

Appendix: Dream Journal

How to use this Dream Journal

This dream journal is based off the protocol outlined by Silva in chapter seven of this book. In order to harness the power of your subconscious, you must first practice recalling your dreams. For this purpose, the first ten days of the journal focus only on recall.

Once basic recall has been established, you can move on to the next section of the journal. Here you will practice using the affirmative statement necessary to produce dreams that contain the answers to specific problems. By actively seeking answers from your subconscious, you will open your mind to communication with a higher power and your dreams will become powerful tools that enable you to understand and solve your problems.

Each journal entry begins with an affirmation. Repeat this affirmation to yourself before falling asleep each night. Keep the journal near the side of your bed. Upon waking, record every detail of your dream that you can remember. The more you use this journal, the more insight and skill you will gain.

Date: _____

"I want to remember a dream. I will remember a dream."

_____
_____
_____
_____
_____
_____
_____
_____
_____
_____
_____

Date: _____

"I want to remember a dream. I will remember a dream."

_____
_____
_____
_____
_____
_____
_____
_____
_____
_____
_____

Date: —————

> *"I want to remember a dream. I will remember a dream."*

_____
_____
_____
_____
_____
_____
_____
_____
_____
_____
_____

Date: —————

> *"I want to remember a dream. I will remember a dream."*

_____
_____
_____
_____
_____
_____
_____
_____
_____
_____
_____

Date: _____

“I want to remember a dream. I will remember a dream.”

_____
_____
_____
_____
_____
_____
_____
_____
_____
_____
_____

Date: _____

“I want to remember a dream. I will remember a dream.”

_____
_____
_____
_____
_____
_____
_____
_____
_____
_____
_____

Date: _____

"I want to remember a dream. I will remember a dream."

_____
_____
_____
_____
_____
_____
_____
_____
_____
_____
_____

Date: _____

"I want to remember a dream. I will remember a dream."

_____
_____
_____
_____
_____
_____
_____
_____
_____
_____
_____

Date: _____

| "I want to remember a dream. I will remember a dream." |

_____
_____
_____
_____
_____
_____
_____
_____
_____
_____
_____

Date: _____

| "I want to remember a dream. I will remember a dream." |

_____
_____
_____
_____
_____
_____
_____
_____
_____
_____
_____

Date: _____

"I want to remember a dream. I will remember a dream."

_____
_____
_____
_____
_____
_____
_____
_____
_____
_____

Date: _____

"I want to remember a dream. I will remember a dream."

_____
_____
_____
_____
_____
_____
_____
_____
_____
_____

Date: _____

> *"I want to remember a dream. I will remember a dream."*

_____
_____
_____
_____
_____
_____
_____
_____
_____
_____
_____

Date: _____

> *"I want to remember a dream. I will remember a dream."*

_____
_____
_____
_____
_____
_____
_____
_____
_____
_____
_____

Date: ———————

"I want to remember a dream. I will remember a dream."

_____
_____
_____
_____
_____
_____
_____
_____
_____
_____

Date: ———————

"I want to remember a dream. I will remember a dream."

_____
_____
_____
_____
_____
_____
_____
_____
_____
_____

Date: _____

> *"I want to remember a dream. I will remember a dream."*

_____
_____
_____
_____
_____
_____
_____
_____
_____
_____

Date: _____

> *"I want to remember a dream. I will remember a dream."*

_____
_____
_____
_____
_____
_____
_____
_____
_____

Date: _____

> *"I want to remember a dream. I will remember a dream."*

_____

_____

_____

_____

_____

_____

_____

_____

_____

_____

Date: _____

"I want to remember a dream. I will remember a dream."

_____

_____

_____

_____

_____

_____

_____

_____

_____

_____

Date: _____

> *"I want to have a dream that will contain information to solve the problem I have in my mind. I will have such a dream, remember it, and understand it."*

Problem: _____

_____

_____

Dream: _____

_____

_____

_____

_____

_____

_____

_____

_____

_____

_____

_____

How does this dream relate to my current problem? What will I do to apply the solution in my life today?

_____

_____

_____

_____

_____

_____

_____

_____

Date: _____

> *"I want to have a dream that will contain information to solve the problem I have in my mind. I will have such a dream, remember it, and understand it."*

Problem: _____

_____

_____

Dream: _____

_____

_____

_____

_____

_____

_____

_____

_____

_____

How does this dream relate to my current problem? What will I do to apply the solution in my life today?

_____

_____

_____

_____

_____

_____

_____

_____

Date: _____

Problem: _____

_____

_____

Dream: _____

_____

_____

_____

_____

_____

_____

_____

_____

_____

_____

_____

How does this dream relate to my current problem? What will I do to apply the solution in my life today?

_____

_____

_____

_____

_____

_____

_____

_____

Date: _____

> *"I want to have a dream that will contain information to solve the problem I have in my mind. I will have such a dream, remember it, and understand it."*

Problem: _____
_____
_____

Dream: _____
_____
_____
_____
_____
_____
_____
_____
_____
_____
_____
_____

How does this dream relate to my current problem? What will I do to apply the solution in my life today?

_____
_____
_____
_____
_____
_____
_____
_____

Date: _____

> *"I want to have a dream that will contain information to solve the problem I have in my mind. I will have such a dream, remember it, and understand it."*

Problem: _____

_____

_____

Dream: _____

_____

_____

_____

_____

_____

_____

_____

_____

_____

_____

How does this dream relate to my current problem? What will I do to apply the solution in my life today?

_____

_____

_____

_____

_____

_____

_____

_____

Date: _____

> *"I want to have a dream that will contain information to solve the problem I have in my mind. I will have such a dream, remember it, and understand it."*

Problem: _____

_____

_____

Dream: _____

_____

_____

_____

_____

_____

_____

_____

_____

_____

_____

How does this dream relate to my current problem? What will I do to apply the solution in my life today?

_____

_____

_____

_____

_____

_____

_____

Date: _____

Problem: _____
_____
_____

Dream: _____
_____
_____
_____
_____
_____
_____
_____
_____
_____
_____
_____

How does this dream relate to my current problem? What will I do to apply the solution in my life today?

_____
_____
_____
_____
_____
_____
_____
_____

Date: _____

Problem: _____

_____

_____

Dream: _____

_____

_____

_____

_____

_____

_____

_____

_____

_____

How does this dream relate to my current problem? What will I do to
apply the solution in my life today?

_____

_____

_____

_____

_____

_____

_____

_____

Date: _____

> *"I want to have a dream that will contain information to solve the problem I have in my mind. I will have such a dream, remember it, and understand it."*

Problem: _____
_____
_____

Dream: _____
_____
_____
_____
_____
_____
_____
_____
_____
_____
_____
_____

How does this dream relate to my current problem? What will I do to apply the solution in my life today?

_____
_____
_____
_____
_____
_____
_____
_____

Date: _____

Problem: _____
_____
_____

Dream: _____
_____
_____
_____
_____
_____
_____
_____
_____
_____
_____

How does this dream relate to my current problem? What will I do to
apply the solution in my life today?

_____
_____
_____
_____
_____
_____
_____
_____

Date: _____

Problem: _____
_____
_____

Dream: _____
_____
_____
_____
_____
_____
_____
_____
_____
_____
_____

How does this dream relate to my current problem? What will I do to apply the solution in my life today?

_____
_____
_____
_____
_____
_____
_____
_____

Date: _____

> *"I want to have a dream that will contain information to solve the problem I have in my mind. I will have such a dream, remember it, and understand it."*

Problem: _____
_____
_____

Dream: _____
_____
_____
_____
_____
_____
_____
_____
_____
_____
_____

How does this dream relate to my current problem? What will I do to apply the solution in my life today?

_____
_____
_____
_____
_____
_____
_____
_____

Date: _____

> *"I want to have a dream that will contain information to solve the problem I have in my mind. I will have such a dream, remember it, and understand it."*

Problem: _____
_____
_____

Dream: _____
_____
_____
_____
_____
_____
_____
_____
_____
_____
_____

How does this dream relate to my current problem? What will I do to apply the solution in my life today?

_____
_____
_____
_____
_____
_____
_____
_____

Date: _____

Problem: _____
_____
_____

Dream: _____
_____
_____
_____
_____
_____
_____
_____
_____
_____
_____

How does this dream relate to my current problem? What will I do to apply the solution in my life today?

_____
_____
_____
_____
_____
_____
_____
_____

Date: _____

> *"I want to have a dream that will contain information to solve the problem I have in my mind. I will have such a dream, remember it, and understand it."*

Problem: _____

_____

_____

Dream: _____

_____

_____

_____

_____

_____

_____

_____

_____

_____

_____

How does this dream relate to my current problem? What will I do to apply the solution in my life today?

_____

_____

_____

_____

_____

_____

_____

_____

Date: _____

> *"I want to have a dream that will contain information to solve the problem I have in my mind. I will have such a dream, remember it, and understand it."*

Problem: _____
_____
_____

Dream: _____
_____
_____
_____
_____
_____
_____
_____
_____
_____
_____

How does this dream relate to my current problem? What will I do to apply the solution in my life today?

_____
_____
_____
_____
_____
_____
_____
_____

Date: _____

Problem: _____

_____

_____

Dream: _____

_____

_____

_____

_____

_____

_____

_____

_____

_____

_____

How does this dream relate to my current problem? What will I do to
apply the solution in my life today?

_____

_____

_____

_____

_____

_____

_____

_____

Date: _____

> *"I want to have a dream that will contain information to solve the problem I have in my mind. I will have such a dream, remember it, and understand it."*

Problem: _____

_____

_____

Dream: _____

_____

_____

_____

_____

_____

_____

_____

_____

_____

_____

How does this dream relate to my current problem? What will I do to apply the solution in my life today?

_____

_____

_____

_____

_____

_____

_____

_____

Date: _____

> *"I want to have a dream that will contain information to solve the problem I have in my mind. I will have such a dream, remember it, and understand it."*

Problem: _____

_____

_____

Dream: _____

_____

_____

_____

_____

_____

_____

_____

_____

_____

_____

_____

How does this dream relate to my current problem? What will I do to apply the solution in my life today?

_____

_____

_____

_____

_____

_____

_____

_____

Date: _____

Problem: _____
_____
_____

Dream: _____
_____
_____
_____
_____
_____
_____
_____
_____
_____
_____

How does this dream relate to my current problem? What will I do to apply the solution in my life today?

_____
_____
_____
_____
_____
_____
_____
_____

Date: _____

Problem: _____

_____

_____

Dream: _____

_____

_____

_____

_____

_____

_____

_____

_____

_____

How does this dream relate to my current problem? What will I do to apply the solution in my life today?

_____

_____

_____

_____

_____

_____

_____

Date: _____

> *"I want to have a dream that will contain information to solve the problem I have in my mind. I will have such a dream, remember it, and understand it."*

Problem: _____

_____

_____

Dream: _____

_____

_____

_____

_____

_____

_____

_____

_____

_____

_____

_____

How does this dream relate to my current problem? What will I do to apply the solution in my life today?

_____

_____

_____

_____

_____

_____

_____

_____

Date: _____

> *"I want to have a dream that will contain information to solve the problem I have in my mind. I will have such a dream, remember it, and understand it."*

Problem: _____

_____

_____

Dream: _____

_____

_____

_____

_____

_____

_____

_____

_____

_____

_____

_____

How does this dream relate to my current problem? What will I do to apply the solution in my life today?

_____

_____

_____

_____

_____

_____

_____

_____

Date: _____

Problem: _____

_____

_____

Dream: _____

_____

_____

_____

_____

_____

_____

_____

_____

_____

_____

How does this dream relate to my current problem? What will I do to apply the solution in my life today?

_____

_____

_____

_____

_____

_____

_____

Date: _____

> *"I want to have a dream that will contain information to solve the problem I have in my mind. I will have such a dream, remember it, and understand it."*

Problem: _____

_____

_____

Dream: _____

_____

_____

_____

_____

_____

_____

_____

_____

_____

_____

How does this dream relate to my current problem? What will I do to apply the solution in my life today?

_____

_____

_____

_____

_____

_____

_____

_____

Date: _____

> "I want to have a dream that will contain information to solve the problem I
> have in my mind. I will have such a dream, remember it, and understand it."

Problem: _____
_____
_____

Dream: _____
_____
_____
_____
_____
_____
_____
_____
_____
_____
_____

How does this dream relate to my current problem? What will I do to
apply the solution in my life today?

_____
_____
_____
_____
_____
_____
_____
_____

Date: _____

Problem: _____
_____
_____

Dream: _____
_____
_____
_____
_____
_____
_____
_____
_____
_____

How does this dream relate to my current problem? What will I do to apply the solution in my life today?

_____
_____
_____
_____
_____
_____
_____

Date: _____

Problem: _____

_____

_____

Dream: _____

_____

_____

_____

_____

_____

_____

_____

_____

_____

How does this dream relate to my current problem? What will I do to
apply the solution in my life today?

_____

_____

_____

_____

_____

_____

_____

Date: _____

Problem: _____

_____

_____

Dream: _____

_____

_____

_____

_____

_____

_____

_____

_____

_____

_____

_____

How does this dream relate to my current problem? What will I do to apply the solution in my life today?

_____

_____

_____

_____

_____

_____

_____

_____

Date: _____

> *"I want to have a dream that will contain information to solve the problem I have in my mind. I will have such a dream, remember it, and understand it."*

Problem: _____

_____

_____

Dream: _____

_____

_____

_____

_____

_____

_____

_____

_____

_____

_____

How does this dream relate to my current problem? What will I do to apply the solution in my life today?

_____

_____

_____

_____

_____

_____

_____

_____

Made in the USA
Columbia, SC
25 July 2024